MCR 22.95

MCR

DEC 1 4 2007

xBiog Xzibit Lemme.M
Lemmens, MaryJo.
Xzibit /

HIP-HOP

Alicia Keys
Ashanti
Beyoncé
Black Eyed Peas
Busta Rhymes
Chris Brown
Christina Aguilera
Ciara
Cypress Hill
Daddy Yankee
DMX
Don Omar
Dr. Dre
Eminem
Fat Joe
50 Cent
The Game
Hip-Hop: A Short History
Hip-Hop Around the World
Ice Cube
Ivy Queen
Jay-Z
Jennifer Lopez
Juelz Santana
Kanye West

Lil Wayne
LL Cool J
Lloyd Banks
Ludacris
Mariah Carey
Mary J. Blige
Missy Elliot
Nas
Nelly
Notorious B.I.G.
OutKast
Pharrell Williams
Pitbull
Queen Latifah
Reverend Run (of Run DMC)
Sean "Diddy" Combs
Snoop Dogg
T.I.
Tupac
Usher
Will Smith
Wu-Tang Clan
Xzibit
Young Jeezy
Yung Joc

Not very many people know the name Alvin Nathaniel Joiner IV—but millions of music fans all over the world know the hip-hop star who today goes by the name Xzibit.

Hip-Hop

Xzibit

MaryJo Lemmens

EVANSTON PUBLIC LIBRARY
CHILDREN'S DEPARTMENT
1703 ORRINGTON AVENUE
EVANSTON, ILLINOIS 60201

Mason Crest Publishers

Xzibit

Copyright © 2008 by Mason Crest Publishers. All rights reserved. No part of this publication may be reproduced or transmitted in any form or by any means, electronic or mechanical, including photocopying, recording, taping, or any information storage and retrieval system without permission from the publisher.

Produced by Harding House Publishing Service, Inc.
201 Harding Avenue, Vestal, NY 13850.

MASON CREST PUBLISHERS INC.
370 Reed Road
Broomall, Pennsylvania 19008
(866)MCP-BOOK (toll free)
www.masoncrest.com

Printed in the United States of America

First Printing

9 8 7 6 5 4 3 2 1

Library of Congress Cataloging-in-Publication Data

Lemmens, MaryJo.
　Xzibit / MaryJo Lemmens.
　　　p. cm.— (Hip-hop)
　Includes index.
　ISBN: 978-1-4222-0305-7
　ISBN: 978-1-4222-0077-3 (series)
 1. Xzibit (Musician)—Juvenile literature. 2. Rap musicians—United States—Biography—Juvenile literature. I. Title.
　ML3930.X95L46 2008
　782.42164902—dc22

2007028141

Publisher's notes:
- All quotations in this book come from original sources and contain the spelling and grammatical inconsistencies of the original text.

- The Web sites mentioned in this book were active at the time of publication. The publisher is not responsible for Web sites that have changed their addresses or discontinued operation since the date of publication. The publisher will review and update the Web site addresses each time the book is reprinted.

DISCLAIMER: The following story has been thoroughly researched, and to the best of our knowledge, represents a true story. While every possible effort has been made to ensure accuracy, the publisher will not assume liability for damages caused by inaccuracies in the data, and makes no warranty on the accuracy of the information contained herein. This story has not been authorized nor endorsed by Xzibit.

Contents

Hip-Hop Time Line	6
1 The Beat and the Rhyme	**9**
2 The Roots	**19**
3 Full Speed Ahead	**29**
4 Second Stardom	**41**
5 Full Circle	**51**
Chronology	56
Accomplishments and Awards	58
Further Reading/Internet Resources	60
Glossary	62
Index	63
About the Author	64
Picture Credits	64

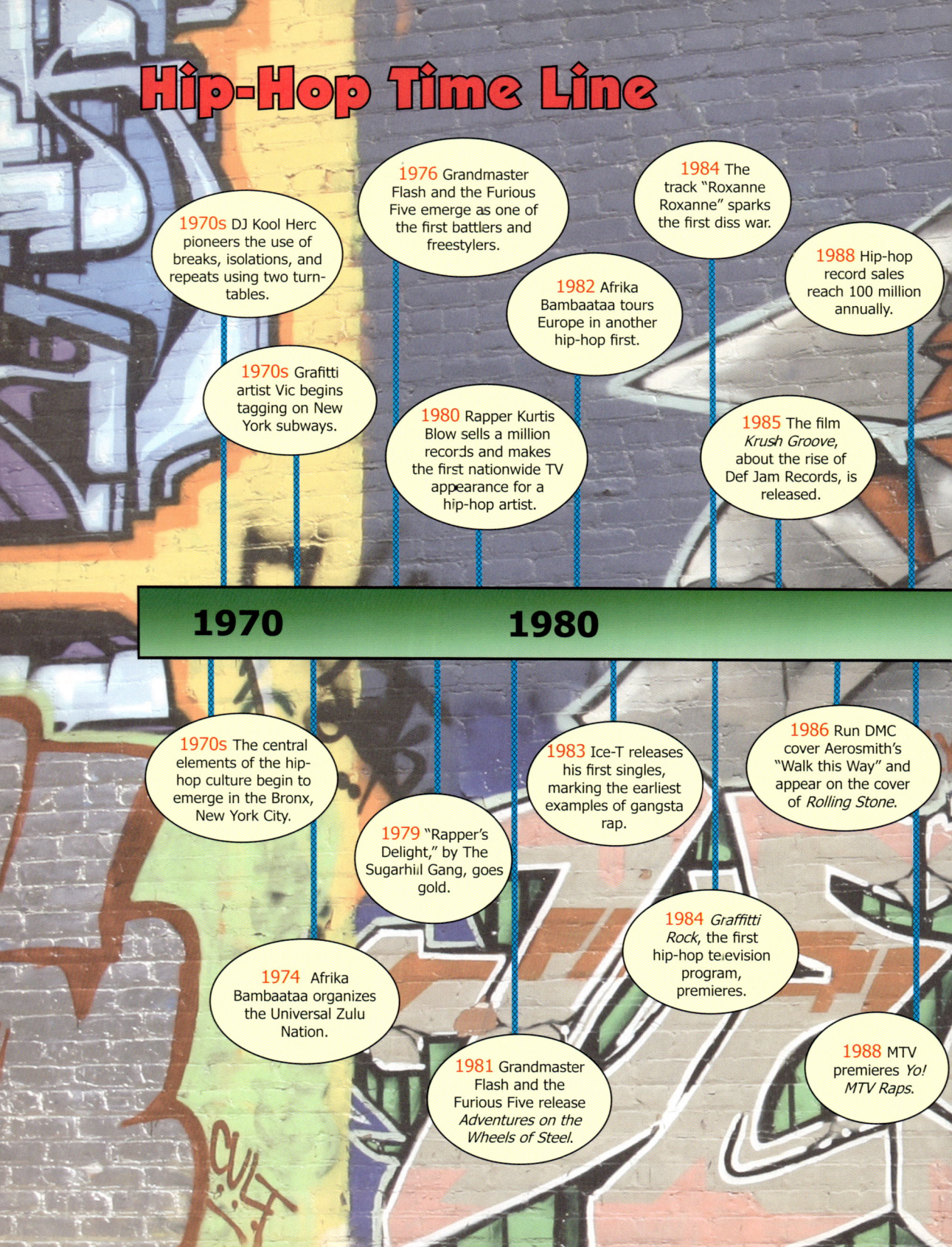

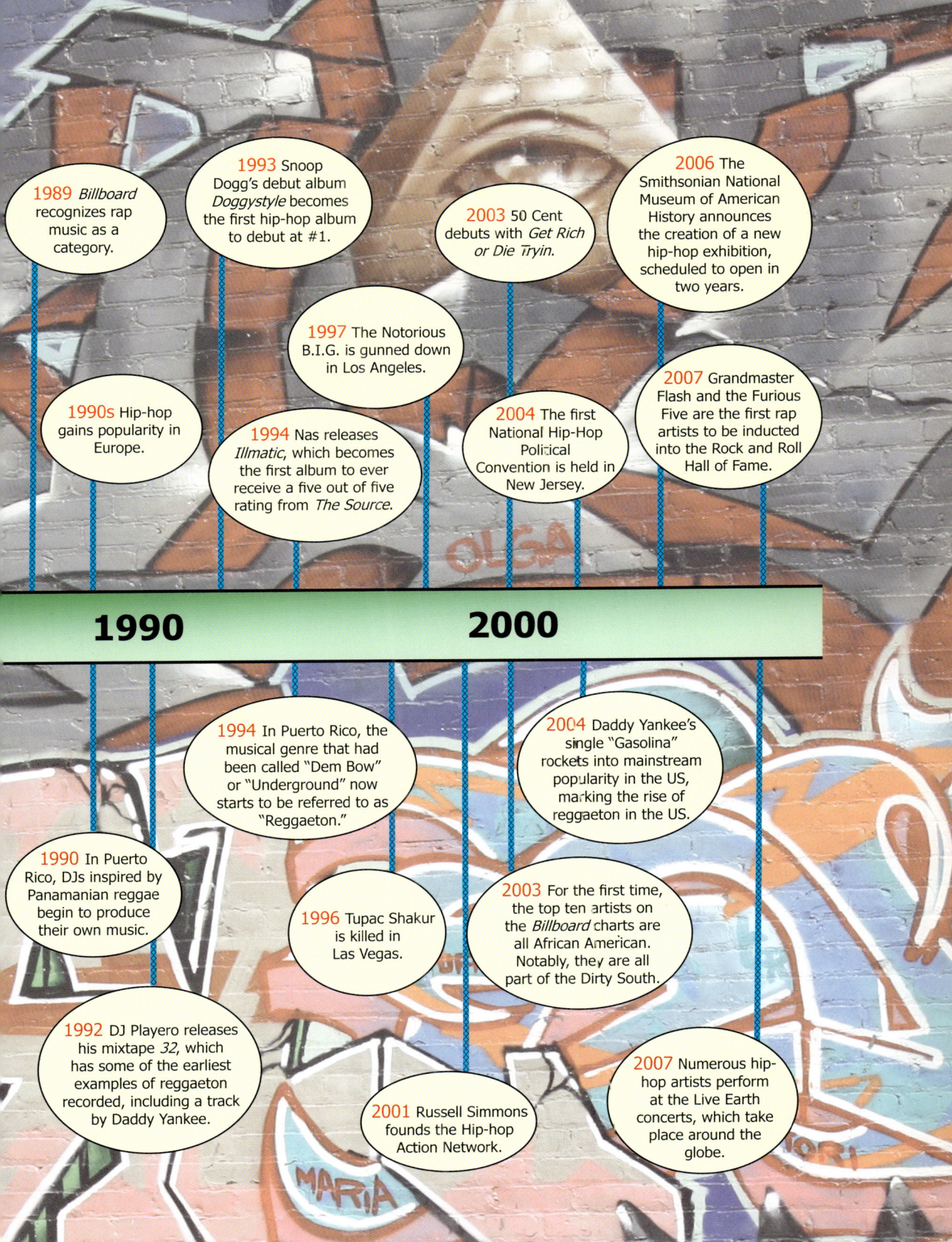

Xzibit is serious when it comes to his music. Hip-hop was born in the streets, and it continues to use rhyme and rhythm to tell the real story of the world.

The Beat and the Rhyme

Hip-Hop on Top

Hip-hop grabs you and doesn't let go. The beat gets into your body, the rhymes get into your brain, and you want to be the music. You want to jump to it, rap with it, throw your fist up in the air and be defiant. It's alive and real, and it moves your soul. The pumping music raises you up, entertains you, inspires you; it allows you to escape and, for a moment, be something different. It is the harsh music of the inner city and the hopeful expression of people's dreams. This music clawed its way out of the ghetto, overcame color lines and class barriers, and became some of the most popular music on earth. Today, millions of people around the world are hip-hop fans, and hip-hop artists are superstars. Xzibit is one of those shining stars in the hip-hop sky.

Hip-hop music and artists like Xzibit are hugely popular, but they are not loved by everyone. Although the music often talks about poverty, inequality, and overcoming difficult circumstances, some hip-hop music is filled with profanity, violence, extreme sexuality, and prejudice, making it the most controversial music around. "Gangsta," "hardcore," and "Dirty South" rap are all forms of hip-hop that have earned reputations for being excessively violent, profane, or sexual, and Xzibit is among the artists making this type of music.

Xzibit, also called "X" or "X to tha Z," is a hardcore, West Coast rapper. He is by no means the most extreme artist around, but his music has its fair share of profanity and controversial subjects. Some people find his uncompromising style a turnoff. Xzibit's fans, however, love his unapologetic grittiness. They say that Xzibit "keeps it real" by making the street's music, rhyming the inner city's poetry. It may be harsh, but according to Xzibit and his fans, it's reality—honest, unfiltered, and un-sold-out. It's also part of a hip-hop tradition of reflecting and commenting on the coarse, urban world from which it evolved.

X to tha Z

Xzibit's rough voice and aggressive rhymes distinguish his music. He has not had the same widespread commercial success as some other hip-hop artists—for example, only one of his albums has broken into the top ten on the *Billboard* 200 album chart—but his albums and singles are very popular on urban radio stations. While Xzibit's name rarely graces the pop charts, it rides high on *Billboard's* Top R&B/Hip-Hop Albums, Hot R&B/Hip-Hop Songs, and Hot Rap Tracks charts. Xzibit also **collaborates** with hip-hop's heaviest hitters. He's worked with rap megastars like Snoop Dogg, Dr. Dre, and Eminem.

Xzibit has a lot of music out there for his fans. He's released six albums since 1996, and although he's not one of

THE BEAT AND THE RHYME

the biggest chart-toppers, he has plenty of loyal fans. They adore his solo work and his collaborations. They see Xzibit as a true rapper—someone who keeps it real and refuses to sell out to pop music and culture. Ironically, his street credibility has increased his mainstream influence. In 2004, his fame skyrocketed when he became the host of MTV's hit show, *Pimp My Ride*. He's also ventured into acting. In 2006, he starred in the film *Gridiron Gang* with Dwayne "The Rock" Johnson, L. Scott Caldwell, and Kevin Dunn. He's also appeared in other films, including *8 Mile*, starring Marshall "Eminem" Mathers and Kim Basinger, and *Derailed*, starring Clive Owen, Jennifer Aniston, and Vincent Cassel.

Though he has a hit television show on MTV and has ventured into films alongside The Rock, Clive Owen, and Jennifer Anniston, music and performing are still important to Xzibit. He loves giving his fans his best every time.

Today Xzibit's music, show, and movies play all over the world, but it's been a hard road to the top. His story, in some ways, is the story of hip-hop itself. In spite of Xzibit's troubled beginnings, he turned his life around when he moved to the West Coast and began a musical career. His aggressive style and explicit lyrics earned him loyal fans and commercial success, but also made him one of hip-hop's more controversial artists.

To fully understand Xzibit's music and message, however, you must understand the history behind hip-hop. Whether people approve of it or not, hip-hop's harsher side has its roots in the grim realities of the world where it was born. Hip-hop today, in all its forms, reflects a history of struggle and rebellion. Hip-hop began as a way for generations of young people

It can be hard to find something uplifting when you live in poverty, when the world around you seems to be in decay. Hip-hop and rap music gave many urban young people an outlet for their frustration.

to express themselves, fight against oppression, and gain respect.

The Burning Bronx

Hip-hop is a cultural movement that was born in the deep, troubled heart of the urban ghetto. It began in the 1970s in the African American and Latino communities of the Bronx in New York City. The Bronx was in decline. Many factors contributed to its deterioration, but one of the largest was an expressway that cut a scar across the city, separating and destroying the neighborhoods in its path. Another was an explosion of high-density housing projects. The projects became failed social experiments that created areas of concentrated poverty and crime.

By the seventies, the people with enough money to do so had fled the changing Bronx neighborhoods. The poorest residents, most of whom were African American or Latino, were left behind to face falling property values, declining schools, and increasing crime. Arsons plagued the borough, especially on the south side, and gave birth to the famous phrase, "The Bronx is burning." It was a harsh world, marred by poverty, crime, and hopelessness. Young people searched for meaning, hope, and a way to express themselves. They wanted recognition and respect, but for poor black and Latino kids in the Bronx, recognition and respect were hard to come by.

The struggle to find pleasure, meaning, and purpose in a depressing, dangerous, and uncertain corner of New York City gave birth to a new form of art and culture. Throughout human history, art has been something people turn to for enjoyment, communication, and inspiration. People can express their deepest thoughts and most complex emotions through art. They can tell people the story of their lives through a poem, a paintbrush, a dance, or a song. Creating, enjoying, and participating in art can lift people from their circumstances and make them part of something better, something greater, something special. Young people in the Bronx in the 1970s didn't have much to look forward to. They didn't have a lot to make them feel great or special. But they started making new forms of art, and their efforts became a cultural revolution that would one day affect music, fashion, language, and cultures all over the world.

The DJs and MCs

In the 1970s Bronx communities, people didn't have much, but they could have fun. Music and dancing were the entertainment of choice, and people gathered in clubs, the streets, and parks to party. DJs were the life of the party, spinning funk, soul, and disco records to keep the people dancing. At block parties or parks, they set up their sound systems and hot-wired streetlamps for power. The lights went out, the music blared, and people gathered for a good time.

There was—and is—more to hip-hop than music. Graffiti has played an important role in the hip-hop world. To some, it might look as though someone vandalized this wall. To others, it's a work of art, an expression of a culture, and as such, it should be appreciated.

THE BEAT AND THE RHYME

DJ Kool Herc is usually given credit for sparking the hip-hop musical movement by introducing a Jamaican style of *cutting* and *mixing* music to his parties. Kool Herc isolated the break—the part of a song that is just the beat, without any words or other instruments—and extended it. The break is the best part of the song for dancing, but it's usually short, maybe only fifteen seconds long. Kool Herc could extend the break by using two turntables, each with a record. By mixing back and forth between the two, he could keep the beat going as long as he liked, allowing partiers to dance on and on. It was a revolutionary innovation, and other Bronx and New York City DJs jumped on board. They elevated turntables to instruments and made spinning records an art form. The better the DJ, the better the party, and soon DJs like Kool Herc, DJ Hollywood, Grandmaster Flash, and Afrika Bambaata were in great demand.

Kool Herc, however, didn't just work the turntables. He also worked the microphone. As the music pumped, he'd *emcee*, entertaining the crowd with jokes, stories, banter, boasts, or anything that came to mind. Soon emceeing, or MCing, became an art form of its own as MCs began speaking with the music in complex rhythms and rhymes. The style became known as rapping, and a good MC and DJ could keep a party going all night long. At first the DJs were the stars of the parties. Later, as MCs honed their craft, rapping would overtake DJing, and the MCs would steal the show.

Another element of hip-hop music was beatboxing, creating drum- and bass-like beats with the human voice. A skilled beatboxer can provide the entire percussion portion of a song using just one instrument: his vocal chords. A group of beatboxers providing the music for an MC's rhymes creates a sound like no other. Although beatboxers never became as famous as MCs and DJs, they too were an important part of hip-hop's development.

Graffiti Crews and B-Boys

Music is perhaps the most well-known part of hip-hop culture, but hip-hop is about more than just music. Another aspect of hip-hop culture is graffiti, or tagging. While many people think that graffiti is just a form of vandalism, those in the know realize that graffiti is part of a whole **underground** movement of expression and rebellion that has become an art.

Tagging began simply as a way to say "I was here." In the beginning, it was just a name or number scrawled on a subway car or city bus. But tagging caught on, and soon just making your mark wasn't enough. The taggings got bigger and more elaborate. Taggers used spray paint to make their works larger and accomplish them faster (they wanted to leave their mark, but they didn't want to get caught in the act), and sometimes they worked in crews. Some taggers became artists, making graffiti that was colorful, complex, and thought provoking. The artistic styles they developed became a strong visual influence on hip-hop culture.

If DJing and MCing were hip-hop's musical expression, and graffiti was its visual expression, then b-boying (also called break dancing) was its physical expression. Break dancing is a highly improvisational, rhythmic, and acrobatic dance form. Break-dancers combined complex footwork with full-body moves, gymnastics, and even martial arts techniques to create a new type of dance that required incredible skill, strength, and power. B-boying became one more element of the hip-hop movement.

Battling It Out

Hip-hop's many forms of expression also became forms of competition—who could tag the most places, who could mix the best music, who could spit the best rhymes, who could break down with the best moves. Today we think of gangs battling with guns, but in the 1970s, gangs of young people, mostly young men, used music, art, and dance to battle for turf and respect. That's not to say that DJing, MCing, graffiti, and break dancing replaced violence in the streets. They certainly did not, and sometimes a score on the stage or dance floor might even be settled with violence later on. But this new art of the ghetto did give young people a way to express themselves and something to take pride in, and the best DJs, MCs, b-boys and b-girls, and graffiti artists earned respect and followers.

Hip-hop was born in the Bronx, but it didn't stay there for long. It spread throughout New York City, then to other cities. Soon it had reached across the country, and each artist and region contributed something new to the music. Regional styles like East Coast and West Coast developed, and rivalries began. East Coast artists were more successful and popular through the eighties, but West Coast artists would dominate the nineties.

By the late eighties, a style of hip-hop called gangsta rap was developing. It started in Philadelphia, but quickly moved to the West Coast and became a defining style of West Coast hip-hop. In the mid-nineties, West Coast rap dominated the hip-hop industry, and rivalries between East and West Coast artists became violent, even ending in some murders. By the end of the decade, the East Coast artists were rising again. In the new millennium, however, they were again overshadowed by the newest regional hip-hop style: Southern rap or Dirty South.

Despite the resurgence of the East Coast and the rise of the Dirty South, West Coast artists like Xzibit remain some of the most popular and influential rappers today. In fact, Xzibit's fame and success took hold in the late nineties, when East Coast artists were reclaiming dominance from the West Coast. That, however, didn't stop Xzibit. He's never been one to worry about popularity or fads. He's made a career out of just being himself.

In the beginning, it seemed as though radio stations and television music networks couldn't run away from hip-hop fast enough. Eventually, the genre's popularity couldn't be denied. Run DMC was the first hip-hop group to have its music played regularly on MTV.

The Roots

Early Years in Detroit

Xzibit's legal name is Alvin Nathaniel Joiner IV. He was born on January 8, 1974, in Detroit, Michigan, a time when hip-hop itself was still in its infancy in the Bronx. Like the Bronx, Detroit was in a state of urban decay with high poverty and crime rates, drug epidemics, and arson.

It was the early eighties, and hip-hop had spread around the country when Alvin began listening to hip-hop. Urban areas all over the United States were experiencing many of the problems faced by the Bronx and Detroit, and their communities related to hip-hop music and its message.

There was a lot going on in the hip-hop world. This urban, street music was now played on the radio, and it started sounding more like the rap we hear today. For the first time, hip-hop artists like Run DMC became famous and commercially successful. The simple rhymes of early rap music were becoming more complex, and distinct **genres** of hip-hop music developed around the country.

West Coast artists were developing an aggressive style of rap, and rappers like Kool Moe Dee and LL Cool J fought each other in wars of words—battles that would become standard in hip-hop in the years to come. The East Coast developed its own hardcore style. Kool G Rap & DJ Polo, for example, became famous for hardcore music that told stories of the street. Many East Coast rappers, like Public Enemy, also became extremely political. During the eighties, DJs also introduced new musical techniques, such as **scratching** and **sampling**. By the end of the decade, subgenres of hip-hop, such as gangsta rap, jazz-rap, and conscious hip-hop, had formed.

Heartbreak and Hip-hop

The hip-hop of the eighties had a big effect on Alvin. Alvin's house had no radio, but he heard hip-hop out on the streets. Like so many other young people, Alvin became an instant fan. Detroit was a tough city for a kid to grow up in, but Alvin's childhood was tougher than most. His mother was a writer, and Alvin learned about creativity by watching her. But when Alvin was nine years old, his mother died. He was just a kid, and he was devastated by the loss and heartache.

About a year after her death, Alvin began following in his mother's footsteps by writing. His writing, however, took a different form—lyrics that he could rap to the rhythms of the street. Alvin was just ten years old, and he was rapping partly to deal with the tragedy of losing his mother. Spitting out rhymes helped him express and cope with his troubled mind and broken heart. He would continue to mourn his mother's death as an adult, rapping about it in his famous autobiographical song "Carry the Weight": "I was at the funeral when it all began . . . I lost sight of my mother at the age of nine."

THE ROOTS 21

The real world isn't always pretty, and neither was hip-hop. Artists like Public Enemy dared to tell the real story of the streets. Sometimes that meant telling stories of violence and death. Sadly, the violence sometimes involved the artists themselves.

Soon after his mother's death, Alvin's father remarried and moved the family to Albuquerque, New Mexico. Alvin continued rapping and listening to hip-hop, but the rest of his life turned upside down. While his skills as a rapper were growing, everything else was spinning out of control. Alvin missed Detroit and had difficulty adjusting to life in New Mexico. Worse yet, he had an unhappy home life, and soon he was

Life on Detroit's streets was rough for young Alvin, especially after his mother died. His neighborhood looked a lot like this one, and the potential for trouble seemed to lurk on every street corner. Sometimes it caught up with Alvin.

getting into serious trouble. His behavior was, by his own account, wild. As a young teen, he was placed in state care in a group home. In "Carry the Weight," he tells of teenage years filled with abuse and anger:

> *"I would forever be hit with anything in reach*
> *Then my father would proceed to go to church and preach."*

A lot of kids, once headed down a dangerous path, never find their way back. There are plenty of sad tales of troubled childhoods leading to broken adult lives. When Alvin was released from custody, it was perhaps the most dangerous period of his life. In that moment, he could go two ways—he could go down the troubled path he'd been on before, or he could work to change his life and make something of himself. In an interview with Tavis Smiley for PBS, Xzibit said that he was lucky and could recognize that he had a choice about his life:

> *"So I was taken out of the home early and had to deal with a certain kind of group home situations. But luckily, I came from a well-educated background. I definitely had some girth about me. And so it was a choice. It was an option. Either I can go down this path or I can learn from this, and become more independent, and go make something of myself."*

The second path would be much harder than the first, but Alvin wanted a better life. He wanted to start his musical career and dreamed of signing a record deal. After saving some money, he traveled to California. It was 1992, and he was just seventeen years old.

The Early Years in California

After getting into trouble as a teenager, Alvin was determined to be a success. Hip-hop was the way he wanted to do it. Music was a powerful force driving Alvin and guiding him through hardship and difficult decisions, but success did not come instantly. By day he worked in a clothing store. By night he did freestyle battles with self-written lyrics. In those early years in California, he used the stage name Xzibit A. The A stood for Alvin. Eventually he would drop the A, becoming Xzibit.

Alvin worked hard to earn enough money, but he spent a lot of time just scraping by. Nevertheless, he stayed out of trouble. While many aspiring (and successful) hip-hop artists took pride in their gang membership and illegal activities like drug dealing, Alvin told Tavis Smiley he was determined to stay off that road:

> "[I realized that] I need to use what I have, in order to get where I need to be. And nothing, nothing good comes easy. You know, nothing worth anything comes easy. So I came out to California at 17. . . . I started working at a little clothing shop and just started writing, and going out to like free-style battles and doing that and just really taking my time. I refused to do anything illegal. And it was just to the point where I had done that and I wanted to try something else. The old way wasn't working. So when I did that, it just progressed, I mean, I'm blessed, I was blessed with the opportunities that I had. But you also have to listen, you know. You have to humble yourself and you have to listen to those voices that guide you."

The anger and hurt from his difficult childhood had led him into trouble early on. Now Alvin tried to channel that energy into his music and use it as a source of inspiration. People soon noticed Alvin's lyrics were full of power and raw emotion, and that he had a talent, energy, and commitment that set him apart from his peers.

Getting People's Attention

Alvin had taken a big risk by moving out to California, but it began paying off when he met Broadway, a West Coast producer. Broadway wanted Xzibit to pair up with Ahlee Rocksta. They'd be called the Shady Bunch and Broadway would produce their record. The plan, however, never got off the ground. Instead, Xzibit and his close friend Pen One began working together, with Xzibit as MC and Pen One as DJ. Pen One and Xzibit soon grabbed people's attention, including, for the second time, Broadway's. While the Shady Bunch had not led to mainstream success, Xzibit's talent prompted Broadway to introduce Xzibit to the L.A. hip-hop group Tha Alkaholiks, who in turn put him in touch with rapper and producer King Tee.

By this time, King Tee was pioneering gangsta rap and building the careers of some of hip-hop's biggest names. He collaborated with Ice Cube, Ice T, Rappin' 4-Tay, B-Legit, and others. In fact, King Tee produced Ice T's early gangsta rap tracks, which have since become classic examples of West Coast hip-hop.

King Tee also founded a West Coast hip-hop collective known as Likwit Crew. Xzibit joined up and worked alongside other members such as the Alkaholiks, the Loot Pack, Defari, Declaime, Montage One, and the Barbershop MC's. Likwit Crew's music featured strong bass and electronics and had a huge influence on the developing West Coast sound. Around this time, Xzibit also appeared on King Tee's *IV Life* album, contributing to the track "Freestyle Ghetto." It was a great learning experience for the young rapper. Spending time in the studio taught him that only hard work and dedication

In California, a new form of rap was hot—gangsta rap. Ice Cube (shown here), Ice-T, and B-Legit were rapping out lyrics that some people felt were offensive to women and way too violent. The rappers responded that they were just telling it like it was.

would produce good music. Being on stage also taught Xzibit the valuable lesson that rapping was not enough. A hip-hop artist had to have a stage presence to succeed.

Xzibit's career was beginning to take flight. In 1995, he toured with Likwit Crew. The next year, he launched his debut solo project, *At the Speed of Life*. The album became an instant underground hit and catapulted Xzibit to the verge of mainstream success. It sold over half a million copies worldwide, and fans were beginning to know Xzibit as the aggressive West Coast rapper who would always "keep it real."

When Xzibit hit California, he also hit on the key to success as a hip-hop artist. Before long, the young star was with a top label and putting out records with the biggest names in rap.

Full Speed Ahead

Record Deal

Xzibit's work with King Tee and Likwit Crew created a buzz in L.A. Soon people were talking about the hard-hitting music of these West Coast artists. Word of their sound reached Steve Rifkind, head of LOUD, a record label that specialized in hip-hop. Rifkind paid attention and, after hearing Xzibit, offered him a deal. The record contract meant that Xzibit would release albums on the same label as major hip-hop acts like Wu-Tang Clan, Big Pun, and Dead Prez.

Signing to Rifkind's label also allowed Xzibit to use LOUD's unique form of marketing. Rifkind developed what he calls The Street Team, a ground-up, "*guerrilla* marketing" approach in which music or other products are distributed locally and reach new people largely by word of mouth. When successful, this

grassroots marketing can turn regional popularity into a national and even international buzz.

The Street Team approach was particularly well suited to hip-hop since, from the beginning, hip-hop music spread by word of mouth and by passing recordings from fan to fan. Most people have a distant relationship with music. Their music comes to them over the radio, from CDs purchased in stores, and from digital tracks downloaded onto computers. But hip-hop's earliest fans lived their music. It didn't come to them over radios or off store shelves. It came to them on the street from people they knew. It didn't require any special instruments or training. Anyone could participate . . . all you needed was a rhythm and a rhyme. Hip-hop fans feel very connected to their music; it's a part of them and they are part of it. That's one of the reasons the guerrilla marketing technique worked so well. People felt connected to the music and were happy to pass it around.

Rifkind's grassroots marketing kept artists like Xzibit connected to the street. They were able to "keep it real" yet still get their message out. They could become popular and successful without selling out to advertisers, images, and big marketing campaigns. The approach worked well with Xzibit's music and message. Fans of his music soon noticed that Xzibit's lyrics dealt with some of the most difficult issues that hip-hop and urban America faced.

The First Album

In 1996, soon after signing his deal with Rifkind, Xzibit released his debut album *At the Speed of Life* on the LOUD label. The work was completed with the help of his friend Pen One, with some songs produced by DJ Muggs of Cypress Hill. The resulting sound, with hard-hitting beats, heavy bass, and sometimes eerie background samples, became an underground hit and helped define West Coast hip-hop for the rest of the

FULL SPEED AHEAD

decade. On his fan site, XzibitCentral.com, Xzibit explains the inspiration behind the album's name:

> "I named the album At the Speed of Life because there's a whole lot of [bad stuff] that [people] go through. I know more [guys] that is off-the-wall crazy, runnin' guns and [stuff] than I know regular Joes that all they want to do is feed their kids. That's their speed. But it's weird how everything is coinciding together,

One of the biggest names in hip-hop is Cypress Hill. In 1996, Xzibit had his chance to work with DJ Muggs of Cypress Hill, shown in this photo. *At the Speed of Life* brought the newcomer rave reviews.

After *At the Speed of Life* was released, there were few artists hotter than Xzibit. His "old" fans were wild about the album. New fans flocked to hear this husky-voiced artist whose hard-hitting style was a welcome change from the usual.

and at the same time is moving in all kinds of different directions."

The record had a fresh approach and met with rave reviews. Xzibit's powerful husky voice and his social message won over new fans. It showed Xzibit as a legitimate hip-hop artist, speaking from the heart. The style emphasized microphone skills and proved he had the talent to be legit; he didn't have to pose as something he was not.

On the album, Pen One produced a song called "Enemies & Friends," and it's a great example of Xzibit's style. It's hard-hitting, dealing with themes he sees all around him, but it also reflects integrity. At one point Xzibit raps "Handle your business / Don't let your business handle you." Later in the song, he offers some tough advice: "Only the strong survive."

The biggest hit on the album was a song about the rap industry called "Papparazi." For Xzibit, music is not a gimmicky sideshow, and in "Papparazi" he criticizes rappers who are more concerned with money and fame than with making real music. The song is part of a long tradition in rap music of looking critically at the music industry and society generally.

Xzibit was pleased with *At the Speed of Life*. On Xzibit-Central.com he is quoted as saying:

"I couldn't pick a better time because what I'm bringin' to the table is fresh and new. I did this album for a lot of reasons other than the flim-flam and the whoopty-whoop, the pictures, the travel and that. This album is heartfelt."

The album hit #74 on the *Billboard* 200 music chart. Among dedicated fans, it climbed even higher, reaching the ninth position on the Hot Rap singles chart. The song "Papparazi" was eventually picked up by Tony Hawk's Pro Skater 3 video game, giving it an even wider audience. Sales of *At the Speed of Life* grew, totaling around 380,000 in the United States and 600,000 worldwide.

The album also earned Xzibit a reputation as a trendsetter. In the song "The Foundation," DJ Muggs provides a haunting loop, incorporating the sound of Xzibit's baby into the song. Xzibit had become a father while working on the album, and the lyrics in "The Foundation" provide an original and emotional message from father to son: "You are the foundation. . . . Gotta live to the fullest never follow behind no man."

Fans and critics loved Xzibit's personal style and how he used hip-hop to channel emotion and meaning. As an MC, he was beginning to control his emotions as well as his mic. The process of making music, Xzibit says, is a release from the anger and aggression that caused so many problems for him in his youth: "I express a lot of anger through writing. I just take my hostility in my thoughts and put it down in a rhyme."

Breaking Down Barriers

At the Speed of Life was released as hip-hop hit new levels of popularity across the United States and the world. MCs had adopted complex rhythms, rapped off-beat, and created new sounds and styles. Producers like DJ Muggs pushed ideas to new levels, sampling sounds that provided emotional landscapes for the MC's words and pushing the music to a new artistic level. West Coast and East Coast rappers dealt with heavy subjects like gang rivalries, street violence, drug abuse, and poverty. Xzibit fit naturally into these new musical trends and contributed to hip-hop's further development.

Hip-hop was also breaking through many social barriers and becoming popular with wider audiences. Once the music of urban black and Latino youths, hip-hop was now crossing color lines and economic barriers. It was the new cultural language of young people, and hip-hop fans could relate to each other even if they came from vastly different backgrounds.

As hip-hop's popularity grew, so did the influence of its culture. Hip-hop crossed cultural lines, appealing to urban young people who were black, Latino, Asian, and Middle Eastern.

So what does a kid in the Bronx, New York, have in common with one living in the OC of California? For many, it's a love of hip-hop—its music, its clothing, and its movement. The hip-hop "look" was as popular as its sound.

For perhaps the first time in history, a poor kid in the inner city was listening to the same music as an upper-class kid in Beverly Hills. It was a revolution that even spread around the world, linking fans in the United States with fans in Asia, Europe, the Middle East, and elsewhere.

Young people's love of hip-hop wasn't just about the music. It was also about the fashion. Kids across the country were wearing baggy pants, expensive running shoes, and oversized shirts. Fashion houses like Tommy Hilfiger and Ralph Lauren picked up on the trend and created hip-hop-inspired clothing lines. In turn, these labels became popular in inner cities. Middle-, lower-, and upper-class young people wore the very same clothes. Fans were expressing their common tastes, regardless of their social background. Hip-hop was topping the charts and shaping lifestyles.

As hip-hop's popularity increased, criticism followed. The criticism came from all sides. Hardcore rappers accused pop-hip-hop artists of "selling out." Many adults criticized the youthful fashions as imitating gangbangers. Inner-city hip-hop fans called wealthier fans "posers" who had no real-life connection to or understanding of the music. But the biggest criticism around, made by some critics, fans, and hip-hop artists alike, was that the hardcore and gangsta styles had gone too far, making music that degraded women, glorified gangs, encouraged violence, and promoted hate and prejudice. Nevertheless, the popularity of even the hardest hitting hip-hop continued to soar straight through the late nineties and into the new millennium.

The West Coast Sound and Controversy

In 1998, Xzibit released *40 Days & 40 Nightz*, which also met with great reviews. The album hit #1 on BET's *Rap City* and stayed there for a record-setting six consecutive weeks.

Sales were lower than with *At the Speed of Life*, but still totaled a respectable 190,000 copies sold in the United States. Worldwide sales totaled 300,000. The album ensured Xzibit a place as one of the best new talents to emerge from the West Coast.

Along with Xzibit, a whole new generation of rappers was becoming famous. West Coast names that he had worked with in the past, including Likwit Crew, were becoming more and more popular. At the same time, other rappers, like Snoop Dogg and Ras Kass, were becoming household names, adored by millions of fans. Working with the legendary Dr. Dre, a Grammy Award–winning producer and former member of NWA, Snoop Dogg released an album on Death Row Records. There is little doubt that Snoop's influence extended from coast to coast. And Snoop's sound influenced Xzibit, who teamed up with him and Dr. Dre to make the nationwide hit "Bitch Please."

If Xzibit had been a wildly successful underground artist up until this point, working with Dre and Snoop gave him the **mainstream** breakthrough he had been searching for. The song had mass appeal, and Xzibit's name was uttered in the same breath as legends Snoop and Dre. But "Bitch Please" also showed hip-hop's darker side. Critics called the hit sexist. The song also highlighted a common problem—profanity-laced lyrics are difficult for radio stations to play; radio stations must delete or bleep out the swear words. But in hardcore rap, the swear words are so plentiful that radio stations sometimes have to bleep entire lines, making the lyrics and rhymes incomprehensible. It's hard for listeners to fall in love with a song when they can't even hear the words.

Not Stoppin' for No One

Even with all the criticism, however, the song was a big hit, and Xzibit's involvement with it gave him more mainstream exposure. Warning labels were plastered on his albums, his lyrics were criticized, and radio stations had to censor his songs, but his popularity continued to grow.

Xzibit enjoyed collaborating with other West Coast artists, and like his solo work, his team efforts resulted in some of the most original sounding rap of all time. In 1999, Xzibit collaborated with Dr. Dre again, this time in the song "Some L.A. Niggaz" on Dre's album *2001*. *2001* was Dr. Dre's second solo project. It was a dark commentary on life, dealing with gangsta rap themes like marijuana, cars, and a love of the streets. Dr. Dre rapped on the album, but his collaborators, including Xzibit, played a huge role. The album hit #2 on the *Billboard* charts and went six-times **platinum**, selling more than 10 million copies worldwide. It also won Dr. Dre a Grammy Award.

By 1999, both through his solo work and his collaborations, Xzibit had become one of the rappers who defined West Coast hip-hop. He still lacked crossover fame, enjoying little airplay on popular radio stations, but his success in urban radio was undeniable. And now he was about to hit the mainstream in a big way. Steve Rifkind, the man who signed Xzibit to his first record deal, sold LOUD Records to music industry giant Columbia Records. As part of Columbia, Xzibit would have access to a huge audience and gain droves of new fans.

With the new millennium came even more success for Xzibit. He opened the new century on tour with some real legends of hip-hop. The question was whether he would be able to keep up the level of success he had achieved by not selling out.

Second Stardom

The Rising Star

The year 2000 was full of promise for Xzibit. He opened the new millennium as part of Dr. Dre's *Up in Smoke* tour. He now had a nation of loyal fans who admired that he never sold out to achieve success. At concerts, they made their appreciation known. When Xzibit took the stage, audience members crossed their forearms. It made the crowd look like a sea of X's. Xzibit had arrived.

The *Up in Smoke* tour put Xzibit on stage with other influential rappers including Ice Cube, Snoop Dogg, Dr. Dre, and Eminem. With some of the biggest names in hip-hop performing, the show drew massive crowds and a large cross-section of young music lovers. *Up in Smoke* confirmed hip-hop's mass appeal, proving that the music had truly become a mainstream sound.

At the moment of hip-hop's greatest popularity, Xzibit released his third solo album, *Restless*. It was produced by Dr. Dre, and it was Xzibit's best-selling album to date. The album went platinum with sales sky-rocketing to 1.5 million in the United States, far outstripping his earlier records. Worldwide sales hit 3 million. The album climbed the charts, hitting #12 on the *Billboard* 200 album chart. The singles "X," "Front 2 Back," and "Get Your Walk On" became huge hits.

A Household Name

"X" became Xzibit's biggest hit. Like his earlier work, it reflected his roots. The third verse shows Xzibit's aggressiveness and that mainstream success has not changed his beliefs:

One of the hottest tickets of 2000 was Dr. Dre's *Up in Smoke* tour. Right up there with the big names of hip-hop was Xzibit. He had earned his place among some of the biggest names in the business, including Eminem.

SECOND STARDOM

"Seem like everybody around me done changed but me / I stand alone on my own two feet."

Xzibit's lyrics remained raw, but his appeal was now mainstream. Xzibit had become a household name. He took his underground sound to audiences around the country on the *Anger Management* tour, keeping it real with his homies Eminem, Snoop, and Dr. Dre.

Faltering Sales

In 2002, Xzibit released his fourth album, *Man vs. Machine*. It features Xzibit at his best and includes collaborations with artists like Ras Kass, Snoop Dogg, Dr. Dre, Nate Dogg (Snoop's cousin), M.O.P., and Eminem. Dr. Dre was the executive producer of the album. *Man vs. Machine* hit #3 on the *Billboard* 200—the highest chart position Xzibit had ever enjoyed.

Despite the albums initial success on the charts, it didn't sell as well as expected. It went gold, selling a respectable 690,000 copies in the United States and 900,000 worldwide, but its numbers fell short of *Restless*. However, Xzibit was not the only artist to see his sales drop off. It seemed that across the hip-hop world, sales were beginning to fall.

The trend continues. In fact, in recent years, hip-hop sales have slipped so much that some people in the industry have started to point to the music's sometimes-offensive language as a possible cause. Critics had been arguing against the sexism and glorified violence in hip-hop for years. It was only in 2000, when sales started to decline, that industry representatives began to listen. Sales are now down 32 percent from their peak, which has many in the music business concerned that the offensive language has gone too far. Racial and sexist lyrics have led some people, like Russell Simmons, founder of Def Jam records, to say that these "extreme curse words" should be erased from broadcasts as a matter of corporate social responsibility.

While some people argue hip-hop's faltering sales are caused by offensive language and content, other people say it's all part of an evolution involving the entire music industry. Today, fewer people are buying albums. Instead, they're going digital, buying their music online and storing it on their computers or iPods. Customers love the freedom of the new digital music world because they can get the songs they want without having to buy entire albums. The technology has revolutionized the music industry.

Still Going Strong

Despite falling sales, Xzibit continued to release commercially and artistically successful albums. While nothing has topped the success of *Restless*, his albums continue to sell hundreds of thousands of copies. Meanwhile, his songs continue to shape musical trends. Two years after *Man vs. Machine*, Xzibit released *Weapons of Mass Destruction* in 2004.

Weapons of Mass Destruction debuted at #43 on the *Billboard* 200, and cracked the top-20 on the Top R&B/Hip-Hop Albums of the year, hitting #19 on that chart. Sales were his lowest yet, at 283,000 copies sold in the United States. But these numbers were still respectable, certifying the album *gold*.

Despite the decent showing in terms of sales, Xzibit was upset at the lack of promotion for the album. It was something that he had noticed with *Man vs. Machine*, and it put him at odds with Columbia Records. By this time, Sony Music had purchased Columbia, and Xzibit felt they weren't giving him the marketing attention necessary to make his albums successful. In an interview with Billboard.com, Xzibit spoke about his faltering sales during 2002 to 2004:

> "I really wasn't happy with the way Sony put out my last two records. There was no marketing or promotion involved. I don't want to be represented like that.

SECOND STARDOM

What goes up must come down. That's the law of gravity—and perhaps of too-successful rap artists. Some in the music business were quick to grab onto the fact that Xzibit's—and hip-hop's—album sales fell in the early 2000s. Techies point out that today's music buyer has other options; they can download individual songs to their mp3 or iPod® players.

XZIBIT

Xzibit wasn't content to rest on his success as a music star. He needed challenge, so he spread his wings. In 2004, he took on the hosting duties of the super-hot MTV automotive makeover show *Pimp My Ride*. The show was even made into a video game, complete with a virtual Xzibit, available from Activision.

> *It was a difference of opinion and I really wanted to get out there and represent my music as strongly as I did everything else."*

Xzibit wasn't going to let his lagging record sales and difficulties with Sony hold him back. Starting in 2002, just as his troubles with Sony were beginning, Xzibit began to branch out into film and television. It won him a whole new set of fans.

Launching a New Career

In 2002, Xzibit moved into uncharted waters as he began appearing in films. He returned to his Detroit roots for his movie debut in the blockbuster *8 Mile*. The film, starring Eminem, is a gritty semi-autobiographical tale about a white kid from a Detroit trailer park who longs to escape from his impoverished life through rap. Having spent much of his childhood in Detroit, and using rap as an escape from his pain, it was a plot line Xzibit could relate to. Xzibit's role was a relatively minor one, but he also made an important contribution to the movie's soundtrack with the song "Spit Shine." The film was popular and exposed Xzibit to a new audience.

In 2004, the same year he released *Man vs. Machine*, Xzibit hosted a new MTV program called *Pimp My Ride*. The show features a team of car experts professionally restoring vintage cars. It is clear Xzibit, an avid car lover, is enjoying his job, and the show's increasing popularity owes a great deal to him. In 2007, *Pimp My Ride* was nominated for Best TV Show at the Annual Urban Music Awards. Xzibit explained to Xzibit-Central.com what the show means to him:

> *"It's not just about the cars anymore. . . . [It is also about] the boost that these kids get in their self-esteem. You can see it in their faces."*

The acting bug had bitten Xzibit. After playing some supporting roles, he was ready for his big role in 2006, when he starred in *Gridiron Gang*. At the film's premiere, Xzibit didn't have some dolled-up babe on his arm, though. He took his son.

SECOND STARDOM

Xzibit has also continued his acting career with several more movies, including the psychological thriller *Derailed*, starring Clive Owen and Jennifer Aniston. He was also in *XXX: State of the Union*, starring Ice Cube, Willem Dafoe, and Samuel L. Jackson. He had his first starring role in the 2006 film *Gridiron Gang*. He played a parole officer and football coach. He was pleased with the role because it allowed him to play a character completely unrelated to hip-hop.

Xzibit's move from hip-hop to Hollywood was not a decision he took lightly. He actually approached acting with skepticism. In his interview with Tavis Smiley on PBS, Xzibit said,

> "My whole stigma about acting was I didn't want to play the stereotypical role. I didn't want to be a buffoon and get into certain aspects of acting. Because you only get offered certain type of roles in Hollywood as a black man, and then second as coming from the genre that I come from . . . as far as the film and television things that come along, I pick and choose those things wisely."

Like his music career, acting was something Xzibit did on his own terms. With a successful musical career behind him, he could afford to be picky with roles, avoiding those that would stereotype him. By "keeping it real" in both his music and his movies, Xzibit maintained his reputation and increased his success.

Xzibit has known a level of success that few in any music genre ever achieve. But he's not letting his success go to his head. Instead, he's branched out, and he's giving back. Xzibit feels an obligation to his fans, and to up-and-coming stars of the music scene.

Back to Basics

In 2006, Xzibit released his sixth album, *Full Circle*, without the backing of a major label. Instead, he chose to put his music out on the Koch Records label, the largest and fastest growing independent record label in the United States. The album hit #50 on the *Billboard* 200 chart and features artists including King Tee, one of Xzibit's original collaborators, and Kurrupt, part of the Dogg Pound Gang.

Xzibit spoke about the album in an interview with Billboard.com:

> "I just want my fans that know me from music and [for] the fans that know me from other genres of entertainment—like the show or the movies—to lend an ear to it."

Koch Records, however, has a smaller distribution network, and sales have been even lower than for Xzibit's other albums. But the news isn't all bad. Working with a smaller label allows Xzibit to keep more creative control. He can market the album however he wants to. He's adopted an approach similar to the guerrilla marketing of his early career with LOUD Records. Critics have given the music good reviews, and some of the songs reflect a more upbeat message, suggesting that Xzibit is comfortable with where he has arrived and finally able to move on from some of his past anger.

In May 2007, Xzibit launched his *Back II Basics* World Tour, which started in Brussels, Belgium. Xzibit will play shows in Germany, Australia, the United Kingdom, New Zealand, and Japan. He also plans to play some shows in the United States. *Back II Basics* marks the first time in over three years that Xzibit has toured. Fan Web sites are abuzz with the possibility of "X to the Z" hitting the street and pounding out some new material.

Xzibit decided to work his love of cars into the tour, kicking off the European leg by participating in the Gumball 3000 Rally, a 3000-mile car rally across Europe. Unfortunately, Xzibit's love of cars got the better of him, and after zooming off on the first day of the trek in his Lamborghini Gallardo, he lost his license for speeding at 160 km/h in a 100 km/h zone (something like 100 mph in a 60 mph zone). His co-driver took over, and team Xzibit continued the journey.

Giving Back

Like many hip-hop artists, Xzibit came from difficult beginnings, yet he rose above his circumstances and achieved incredible success. Today, Xzibit is trying to give back by making a positive contribution to hip-hop and the world. Through *Pimp My Ride*, the West Coast rapper gives kids in Southern California a chance to turn their beat-up old cars into the

FULL CIRCLE

Xzibit likes acting, and he's good at it. He has proven that he can play characters other than rap stars on the silver screen. His son better get used to premieres and paparazzi!

pimpest rides in the hood. In 2003, Xzibit also founded Rhyme Night, where signed and unsigned acts can come show their skill. With some shows headlined by names like Ras Kass and Xzibit himself, the event draws a big audience and even gets airplay. It gives West Coast hip-hop talent a chance to shine.

Recently, Xzibit used *Pimp My Ride* to raise awareness about environmental issues. He devoted a special Earth Day episode to cars powered with alternative fuels. The episode

Author, businessman, music mogul, humanitarian: these words all describe Russell Simmons. He has been involved in hip-hop since its earliest days, and he has witnessed the music and lifestyle get a bad reputation. Through HSAN, he hopes to help change people's attitudes about hip-hop—and encourage artists to tame their language.

featured a 1965 Chevrolet Impala, restored and souped up with an 800 horsepower Duramax diesel engine that could run on biodiesel fuel. It was classic *Pimp My Ride* with a green twist. The hugely popular show taught many devoted car lovers about earth-friendly fuels.

California governor Arnold Schwarzenegger became an instant fan of the *Pimp My Ride* green initiative. He applauded Xzibit's show for drawing attention to environmental issues. Schwarzenegger appeared in the Earth Day episode and praised the show:

> "I would like to thank MTV and the entire *Pimp My Ride* crew for shining the spotlight on the importance of alternative fuels and the fight against global warming. I am very encouraged by the great potential in converting vehicles to run on biodiesel as a way to reduce greenhouse gas emissions."

The governor didn't just like the idea of the show; he also liked the results. Impressed with the reworked Impala, Schwarzenegger decided to beef up his own street cred. He asked the *Pimp My Ride* mechanics to turn their tools on his big Hummer and deliver the same earth-friendly bang to his ride.

Xzibit has also participated in the work of the Hip-Hop Summit Action Network (HSAN), probably the most well-known charitable organization operating in the hip-hop scene today. Founded by Russell Simmons, HSAN works with at-risk youth across the United States, attempting to improve education and address social issues.

In addition to his charitable work, Xzibit plans to continue making music. His acting career looks nothing but promising, and no matter what happens to hip-hop in the future, Xzibit will be on the cutting edge.

CHRONOLOGY

1970s Hip-hop begins in the Bronx section of New York City.

Jan. 8, 1974 Alvin Nathaniel Joiner IV—Xzibit—is born.

late 1980s Gangsta rap develops.

1990s West Coast artists dominate hip-hop.

1992 Xzibit moves to California.

1995 Xzibit tours with Likwit Crew.

1996 Xzibit's debut album, *At the Speed of Life*, is released.

1998 *40 Dayz & 40 Nightz* is released.

1999 Xzibit collaborates with Dr. Dre on "Some L.A. Niggaz."

2000 Xzibit tours with Dr. Dre's *Up in Smoke* tour. *Restless* is released.

2001 Xzibit appears in *The Wash*.

2002 *Man vs. Machine* is released. Xzibit appears in *8 Mile*.

2003 Xzibit establishes Rhyme Night.

2004 Xzibit becomes the host of MTV's *Pimp My Ride*.

CHRONOLOGY

Weapons of Mass Destruction is released.

Xzibit appears in *Full Clip*.

2005 Xzibit appears in *Derailed and XXX: State of the Union*.

2006 Xzibit costars in *Gridiron Gang* and lends his voice to *Hoodwinked*.

Full Circle is released.

2007 *Pimp My Ride* is nominated for Best TV Show at the Annual Urban Music Awards.

Xzibit participates in the Gumball 3000 Rally.

Jul. 7, 2007 Xzibit performs at the Japanese venue of the Live Earth concert.

ACCOMPLISHMENTS AND AWARDS

Albums

1996   *At the Speed of Life*

1998   *40 Dayz & 40 Nightz*

2000   *Restless*

2002   *Man vs. Machine*

2004   *Weapons of Mass Destruction*

2006   *Full Circle*

Films

2001   *The Wash*

2002   *The Country Bears*
               8 Mile

2004   *Full Clip*

2005   *Derailed*
               XXX: State of the Union

2006   *Gridiron Gang*
               Hoodwinked

DVDs

2000 *The Up in Smoke Tour*

2001 *X.O. The Movie Experience*
Restless Exposed

Awards and Recognition

2007 *Pimp My Ride* is nominated for Best TV Show at the Annual Urban Music Awards.

Books

Bogdanov, Vladimir, Chris Woodstra, Steven Thomas Erlewine, and John Bush (eds.). *All Music Guide to Hip-Hop: The Definitive Guide to Rap and Hip-Hop.* San Francisco, Calif.: Backbeat Books, 2003.

Cabrera, Marc. "Star of 'Pimp My Ride' a Household Name." *Monterey County Herald* (Monterey, Calif.), October 31, 2006.

Chang, Jeff. *Can't Stop Won't Stop: A History of the Hip-Hop Generation.* New York: Picador, 2005.

Kenon, Marci. "'Underground' Label Suits Xzibit." *Chicago Sun-Times*, February 26, 2001.

Kusek, Dave, and Gerd Leonhard. *The Future of Music: Manifesto for the Digital Music Revolution.* Boston, Mass.: Berkley Press, 2005.

Light, Alan (ed.). *The Vibe History of Hip Hop.* New York: Three Rivers Press, 1999.

Mugan, Chris. "Rock and Pop: 'Rap Needs a Message'; Less 'Junk Food,' More Integrity Is Xzibit's New Mantra." *The Independent* (London, England), December 31, 2004.

FURTHER READING/INTERNET RESOURCES

Web Sites

Pimp My Ride
www.mtv.com/ontv/dyn/pimp_my_ride/series.jhtml

Xzibit
www.xzibit.com/main

Xzibit Central
www.xzibitcentral.com

Xzibit on My Space
www.myspace.com/xzibit

Glossary

collaborates—Works with others to achieve something.

cutting—Manually lining up duplicate copies of the same record in order to repeatedly play the same passage.

emcee—Master of ceremonies (MC).

genres—Categories that artistic works can be divided into on the basis of form, style, or subject matter.

gold—A designation that a recording has sold 500,000 copies.

grassroots—The ordinary people in a community.

guerrilla—Something done in an unexpected manner.

mainstream—The ideas, actions, and values that are most widely accepted by a group or society.

mixing—Blending sounds from different sources to come up with a new sound.

platinum—A designation that a recording has sold at least 1 million copies.

sampling—To use a segment of another's musical recording as part of one's own recording.

scratching—Running a record backward and forward on a turntable to repeat and distort the original sound.

underground—Separate from the prevailing social or artistic environment.

Index

At the Speed of Life 27, 30–34, 37

Back II Basics tour 52
Billboard 10, 33, 39, 42, 43, 44, 51

Derailed 11, 49
Detroit, Michigan 19, 20, 22, 47
Dr. Dre 10, 38, 39, 41, 42, 43

8 Mile 11, 47
Eminem 10, 11, 41, 42, 43, 47

40 Days & 40 Nightz 37
Full Circle 51

Gridiron Gang 11, 48, 49

hip-hop
    breaking barriers 33–37
    history 13–17
    West Coast 37–39

Likwit Crew 25, 27, 29, 38

Man vs. Machine 43, 44, 47
MTV 11, 18, 46, 47, 55

New York City 12, 14, 16, 32, 36, 46, 48

Pimp My Ride 11, 47, 52, 54, 55

Restless 41, 43, 44

Snoop Dog 10, 38, 41, 43

Up in Smoke tour 41, 42

Weapons of Mass Destruction 44

Xzibit
    as actor 11, 47–50
    in California 23–28
    early life 19–27
    giving back 52–55
    success 29–34, 37–47

About the Author

MaryJo Lemmens is a children's nonfiction writer who lives in Toronto, Ontario, Canada's largest city. Before moving to Toronto, she lived in the United States and South Africa. She received her bachelor's degree from Smith College in Northampton, Massachusetts. She has written numerous publications for young people.

Picture Credits

Akasha Multimedia / PR Photos: p. 54
Bielawski, Adam / PR Photos: pp. 11, 32
Gabber, David / PR Photos: p. 28
Harris, Glenn / PR Photos: pp. 2, 48
Hatcher, Chris / PR Photos: front cover, pp. 8, 50, 53
iStockphotos:
    Harmon, Steve: p. 14
    Mitic, Slobo: p. 45
    Stalman, Tyler: p. 35
    Thomas, Ben: p. 22
    Whitman, Cameron: p. 12
    Yakovlev, Alexander: p. 36
Kirkland, Dean / PR Photos: p. 40
Mayer, Janet / PR Photos: p. 22
Moore, Anthony G. / PR Photos: p. 26
PR Photos: pp. 18, 31
Thomson, Terry / PR Photos: p. 42
VG Core: p. 46

To the best knowledge of the publisher, all other images are in the public domain. If any image has been inadvertently uncredited, please notify Harding House Publishing Service, Vestal, New York 13850, so that rectification can be made for future printings.